Twenty-First Century **Faith**

Evide
for G

Seven reasons to believe in the existence of God

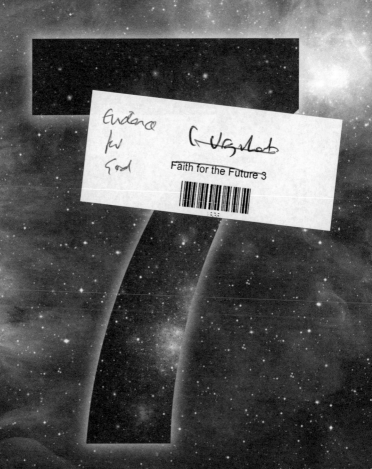

Evidence
for
God

Faith for the Future 3

Andrew Christofides

DayOne

© Day One Publications 2010
First Edition 2010

Unless otherwise indicated, Scripture quotations in this publication are from the New
International Version (NIV), copyright ©1973, 1978, 1984, International Bible Society.
Used by permission of Hodder and Stoughton, a member of the Hodder Headline Group.
All rights reserved.

British Library Cataloguing in Publication Data available

ISBN 978-1-84625-225-9

Published by Day One Publications
Ryelands Road, Leominster, HR6 8NZ

☎ 01568 613 740
FAX: 01568 611 473
email—sales@dayone.co.uk
web site—www.dayone.co.uk
North American e-mail—usasales@dayone.co.uk
North American web site—www.dayonebookstore.com
All rights reserved

Designed by Wayne McMaster and printed by Orchard Press (Cheltenham) Ltd

CONTENTS

ENDORSEMENTS

'The New Atheism' is on the march today, flooding the media with its core message that God does not exist. But is this the case? As a well-qualified scientist, Dr Andy Christofides makes it crystal clear that we are surrounded by evidence that points in exactly the opposite direction. What is more, he shows that in our own physical, mental and spiritual make-up each one of us possesses equally powerful evidence for God. Here is a book to confront the atheist, challenge the sceptic, and confirm the faith of the believer as he or she faces New Atheism's energetic but empty claims.

Dr John Blanchard, Author, Apologist and Conference Speaker

Andy shows that there is no excuse for not believing in God. The Psalmist who wrote some three thousand years ago about the fool saying in his heart there is no God is still right today. It is only a fool that would say there is no God when the evidence for the existence of God is so overwhelming. I have pleasure in commending this book.

Dr A J Monty White, BSc, PhD, CChem, MRSC, Author and Speaker, Biblical Foundations

With clear thinking, concise writing and compelling arguments, Andy Christofides leads us from creation to Christ.

Gary Benfold, Pastor, Moordown Baptist Church, Author of *Reach out for him*

Atheists are becoming more and more strident and zealous in their determination to convince the world of their message: 'There is no God.' Yet, it seems, the more they shriek, the less the general public believes them. After decades of activity by the 'no God' evangelists—including such superstars as Richard Dawkins, Christopher Hitchens and Richard Starkey—the numbers believing in God continue to hold up.

We are being bombarded on TV and radio, in newspaper and magazine articles that God does not exist and that 'Big Bang' and evolution are the facts—yet there are many who still believe in God, and when it comes to evolution, a survey conducted to coincide with Darwin's anniversaries (200 years since his birth and 150 years since the publication of *The Origin of the Species*) over half the British population were found not to believe in Darwinism!

So desperate have some atheists become, they have poured a substantial sum of money into an advertising campaign to press home their message. Many buses throughout Britain have been plastered with this slogan, 'There's probably no God … now stop worrying and enjoy your life.'

The choice of the word 'probably' is an interesting one. Why 'probably'? Are they convinced or aren't they? And, how probably is that? Very probably; quite probably? Fairly probably? I guess an unqualified 'probably' leaves it somewhere in the middle of the range!

And what of the strange conclusion to the slogan; '… now stop worrying and enjoy your life'? What an odd conclusion to draw from the non-existence of a Divine Being, because, if they are right, far from being a relaxing thought, we are at the blind whim of cosmic chance! There would be no reason for our existence and no reason why we should continue. At any time a lump of cosmic rock could hit our planet and we would be gone. The thought that no intelligent Being is in control, that we are without a pilot, hurtling at 66,000 mph around a massive million-mile diameter fusion reactor does NOT make me feel relaxed!

Popular atheism received a major jolt in 2004 when Anthony Flew, a well-known and notorious atheistic philosopher, announced his conversion to theism. On 9th December of that year, the Associated Press story stated, 'A British philosophy professor who has been a leading champion of atheism for more than half a century has changed his mind. He now believes in God more or less based on scientific evidence … '[1]

In 2007 Flew published a book entitled *There is a God* where he outlines the story of his conversion—in it he states:

> I must stress that my discovery of the Divine has proceeded on a purely natural level, without any reference to supernatural phenomena. It has been an exercise in what is traditionally called natural theology. It has no connection with any of the revealed religions. Nor do I claim to have had any

personal experience of God or any experience that can be called supernatural or miraculous. In short, my discovery of the Divine has been a pilgrimage of reason and not of faith.[2]

It would seem that Richard Dawkins was so rattled by this 'conversion' that he suggests in his book *The God Delusion* that Flew's old age was perhaps to blame![3]

In the following chapters, I want to take up the evidence that many have found so compelling. In fact, the evidence for God is so powerful as to leave atheists 'legless'! There are certain fundamental questions that are utterly void of any cogent logical answer without the

There are certain fundamental questions that are utterly void of any cogent logical answer without the existence of God.

existence of God. It is perhaps not surprising that atheists are getting more strident with their arguments. It is often the case that where the argument is weak, the tactic of shouting louder is used!

Our approach here will be calm and measured. The first five chapters cover what could be called 'objective evidences for God'—or what Flew called 'natural theology'. But, I wish to take you beyond that point and into a real encounter with the God who is there—this will be covered in the final two chapters.

Although I have a strong scientific background, this book is aimed at 'the person in the street'. If you have no scientific background and find you can't understand this book, then I have failed in my objective!

For convenience and help in remembering these chapters, each begins with the letter 'C'—so we will have seven 'C's for the existence of God. It has to be admitted, at the outset, that there is no proof for God and it is in the final analysis a matter of faith—but it is my hope that you will find these chapters to be 'powerful pointers' to faith!

1 *The Guardian*; 1st February 2009, www.guardian.co.uk

2 *There Is A God*; Anthony Flew; Harper One; p93 (ISBN 978-0-06-133529-7)

3 *The God Delusion*; Richard Dawkins; Bantam Press; p82 (ISBN 978-0-59-305548-9)

Introduction

Creation

Of all the so-called objective evidences for God, the existence of the universe is by far the most compelling. Let's consider some basic facts about our known universe:

The planet on which we live is travelling at 66,000 mph around a star at a distance of 93 million miles. The solar system has a diameter of around 7,000 million miles, the outermost planet being Neptune. (Pluto was relegated to the lower division in 2005!) The distances are mind-boggling. To travel from earth to the sun in a fast car at 150 mph, would take 71 years!

If you travelled to Neptune and looked back towards the sun, it would be a tiny pinpoint of light and the earth would be an invisible speck.

A LITTLE DOT IN SPACE

In our family of stars (a galaxy called the Milky Way) there are thought to be around 200,000 million other stars. Our nearest neighbouring star is Proxima Centauri, four light years away. (A light year is the distance light travels in a year—about 6 trillion miles—in numerals, that is 6,000,000,000,000 miles). That same fast car would take 20 million years to reach Proxima Centauri!

The Milky Way is thought to be 100,000 light years in diameter. Even Jean-Luc Picard in the star ship *Enterprise* has only been able to explore the alpha quadrant of our galaxy!

Our nearest galactic neighbour of any note is Andromeda,

about 2.3 million light years away and containing about one trillion stars. Andromeda and the Milky Way are not alone—the known universe is thought to contain about 100,000 million other galaxies.

Where did all this come from?

The most popular current theory is the so called 'Big Bang', which, briefly, may be described as follows:

About 13.8 billion (13,800,000,000) years ago, the universe that we now know and see was crammed into a point so small that it would pass through the eye of the finest needle. (Scientists have calculated that the diameter of the universe at that point would have been 0.00000000000000 00000000000000000001 meters; this is known as a Planck length!) Everything was in there—all the matter and energy in the universe today was in that tiny, specky dot. Outside of that dot, there was nothing—not even space, for space itself was in the dot! Then, quite suddenly, due to 'perturbations in the quantum fuzz' (as cosmologists put it!), the whole universe began to emerge in a cosmic big bang. At the point of the big bang, the temperature of the universe was immense—100,000,000,000,000,000,000,000,000,000,000 degrees!

It is not the purpose of this book to examine and explore the evidence for that theory, for those who wish to know more there are many excellent books on this theme including

Stephen Hawkins's *A Brief History of Time*.[1] The problem with the theory is this: it doesn't answer the question, 'Where did it all come from?' If it was a big bang from a tiny dot, where did the dot come from? And science has no answer—not because of any fault in science, but because it would simply be beyond the remit and boundaries of science to answer that question. You see, science can answer questions such as, 'What is it?' and 'How does it work?', but cannot say for certain who made it or why it was made.

For example: If a group of scientists and engineers went into a room and found a cake on a table, they could tell you lots about the cake: the fat and sugar content; the sheer forces between the layers, etc. But they could not tell you who made it, or why it was made. That is not a failing of science; it is simply not fair to ask science such questions. We ask those questions of the cook, who enters the room to tell the scientists, 'I made it for my son Johnny's birthday!'

The universe is truly mind-bogglingly awesome—the more we probe and discover, the more awestruck we become. The pictures transmitted from the Hubble telescope are breathtaking and we understand much of what the universe is and much of how it works ... but as to where it came from and why it is here—science is unable to answer such questions. Ask a scientist, 'Where did the dot come from?' and you will not get a scientific answer! Scientists will either be honest and admit total ignorance, or they will become philosophers and start to relate their feelings on the matter. The ideas being propounded by some scientists border on being mystical or, at best, a scientific philosophy! (For example you could spend some time reading the works of men such as Anthony Zee[2] or Victor Stenger[3].)

There are, however, only three possible categories of answer; and broadly speaking they are as follows:

1. The universe made itself out of nothing.
2. The universe has always been there—it is eternal.
3. An Intelligent Eternal Being (God) made it.

There is no other possibility.

Thankfully, we are able to analyse the first two options in a scientific manner to see if they are possible.

MADE FROM NOTHING

Firstly, the universe made itself out of nothing. How does this hold up to scientific scrutiny? Science has discovered certain fundament laws which operate throughout the universe and which cannot be broken. One of those laws is known as 'the first law of thermodynamics'. There is no need for you to worry about such a big word; the law simply states: 'Energy can neither be created nor destroyed; it can be merely changed into one form or another.'

There are many forms of energy in the universe—heat, light, sound and physical 'stuff' or matter. Simply put, matter is concentrated energy. This can be clearly illustrated by thinking of a lump of coal. By burning coal, you do not 'destroy' the energy in the coal; you simply transform it into other kinds of energy (heat, light, sound) and the total sum of energy remains the same. For this reason the first law of thermodynamics is also known as 'the law of the conservation of energy'.

Now, on the question of the origin of the universe, this law states that it cannot have made itself! Energy can neither be created nor destroyed. The universe cannot have made itself. That is not a matter of speculation—it is a matter of scientific fact. And we all knew that anyway, didn't we? The words sung in the movie *The Sound of Music* where Maria (Julie Andrews) and Captain Von Trapp (Christopher Plummer) continue to resonate: 'Nothing comes from nothing—nothing ever could ... '

Energy can neither be created nor destroyed. The universe cannot have made itself.

However, it is at this point that a number of scientists have ventured into the realms of 'scientific mysticism', speculating that the universe did indeed emerge from 'nothing', not because of any scientific evidence, but because they feel they must say something on the matter!

Most of their arguments revolve around 'symmetry' or

'balance'—everything in the universe is finely balanced between positive and negative, or repulsion and attraction; and since the sum totals are in a balance of almost nothing, it stands to reason, they say, that they could well have emerged from nothing. Even Stephen Hawking has felt it necessary to make his views known on this matter; here is a direct quote from his recently published book *The Grand Design*:

> Because there is such a law as gravity, the universe can and will create itself from nothing ... spontaneous creation is the reason why there is something rather than nothing, why the universe exists, why we exist. It is not necessary to invoke God to light the blue touch paper and set the universe going.[4]

Here Hawking sets matter as positive energy and gravity as negative energy—stating since the two are roughly in balance the universe can create itself! Here is a further extract:

> Because gravity shapes space and time, it allows space-time to be locally stable but globally unstable. On the scale of the entire universe the positive energy of matter can be balanced by the negative gravitational energy, and so there is no restriction on the creation of whole universes.[5]

Hawking's argument is clear: because the universe is there, it must have come from nothing ... by itself.

Well, this is far from the science most of us are familiar

with and seems closer to eastern mysticism. I have Buddhist friends who talk on surprisingly similar lines!

AN ETERNAL UNIVERSE

The second option is that the universe is eternal, that it has always been around, and therefore we have no need to speculate as to its origins. Again, thankfully we can examine this in a scientific manner. There are several laws of thermodynamics; we have looked at the first law, and now we will consider the second law which states: 'The entropy in a closed system is always increasing.'

Perhaps that sounds complicated, but, stated another way it is really quite simple: 'The energy available within any closed system for carrying out useful work is always decreasing.'

We find that rechargeable batteries 'run down' and need recharging. We find that hot coals cool down; water in a hydroelectric power station runs downstream and never back up. Useful, useable energy runs out in any closed system— someone needs to come from the outside to 'top it up' again.

Now, I hope you can see the inference. The universe is a closed system, and in that closed system the energy available for doing useful work is decreasing. From this we can conclude, not from speculation, but from scientific fact, that the universe cannot be eternal.

AN INTELLIGENT BEING

This leaves us with the third option—an Intelligent Being (God) made the universe.

He is pure spirit—an incredibly simple form of existence! He creates the universe, from nothing, by an act of pure spiritual power. He is eternal, timeless, self existent and self sufficient. This is part of who he is by definition. But still the question is often asked: 'Where did God come from; who made him?' or, 'If the universe can't be eternal, how come God can be eternal?'

With the universe, we can (and must) apply the laws of science; with God, however, we cannot—he is not governed by the laws of science; rather, he made those laws to govern his universe!

God is eternal—no one made him. This is not a matter for scientific scrutiny. However, neither is it 'unscientific'. Rather, it is simply beyond the remit of science!

So, when it comes to a consideration of the origins of the universe, there are only three possible options. In looking at those options scientifically, the only logical option is that an Intelligent Being (God) made it out of nothing by an act of pure spiritual power.

When we read the Bible, interestingly, this is exactly what we find. The opening statement of the Bible is: 'In the beginning God created the heavens and the earth.'[6]

The Hebrew word for 'created' is a word meaning 'to create from nothing'. (So, in that sense men such as Stenger and Zee are right—the universe did in fact come from nothing!)

The Bible then points to the universe itself as being a great signpost to tell us that God exists!

For example:

> The heavens declare the glory of God;
>> the skies proclaim the work of his hands.

> Day after day they pour forth speech;
>> night after night they display knowledge.

> There is no speech or language
>> where their voice is not heard.

> Their voice goes out into all the earth,
>> their words to the end of the world.[7]

The universe is, as it were, a great banner unfurled by God, speaking urgently and relentlessly to us, 'There is a God'. So clear is that banner that the Apostle Paul, in his letter to a church in Rome, states that this evidence leaves us, 'without excuse' if we fail to recognize him![8]

It is reported that the late Sir John Mortimer (author of *The Rumpole of the Baily* series) loved to debate the existence of God with bishops, taunting them that their 'evidence was deficient'.[9]

My learned reader—in considering the evidence for God, it is far from deficient. I give you 'Exhibit A'—the universe!

1 *A Brief History of Time*; Stephen Hawking; Bantam Press (ISBN 0-593-01518-5)

2 *Fearful Symmetry*; Anthony Zee; MacMillan Publishing (ISBN 0-02-633430-5)

3 *God—The Failed Hypothesis*; Victor Stenger; Prometheus Books (ISBN 978-1-59102-652-5)

4 *The Grand Design* by Stephen Hawking and Leonard Mlodinow; (ISBN 978-0-7393-4426-2)

5 Ibid.

6 Genesis 1:1

7 Psalm 19:1–4

8 Romans 1:18–20

9 *The Times*: 23rd January 2009

Creation

Coincidence

The more we consider the universe, the more we discover about its workings, and the more we are drawn to the conclusion that it is finely tuned and ordered to allow us to exist!

These are not just the thoughts of religious people. Many agnostic scientists have made similar comments; for example, Stephen Hawking has written the following:

> The laws of science, as we know them at present, contain many fundamental numbers, like the size of the electric charge of the electron and the ratio of the mass of the proton and the electron ... The remarkable fact is that these numbers seem to have been finely adjusted to make possible the development of life. For example if the electric charge of the electron had been only slightly different, stars either would have been unable to burn hydrogen and helium, or else they would not have exploded.[1]

Are these things coincidences of blind cosmic chance, or are they designed by an Intelligent Being? In this chapter we will be considering just a few of these 'coincidences' which are vital to our life here on planet earth.

WATER

As I write this chapter, water is pouring down from the sky onto the west Wales coastline and waves are crashing onto the beach while nearby a river runs carrying water from the hillsides into the sea. Water, water, everywhere! Without it, life (as we know it) is impossible. Our bodies are 65% water; we need it—and thankfully the earth has plenty of it; about 65% of the surface of the earth is covered in water.

But, it is not the presence of water that I want to comment on—rather its amazing properties.

First of all, it is amazing that water is a liquid at all. Water, chemically, is two atoms of hydrogen (a gas) joined to one atom of oxygen (also a gas). Put together in a water molecule (H_2O), they form a liquid! Other comparable molecules to water, such as hydrogen sulphide (H_2S) and hydrogen cyanide (HCN), are gases at room temperatures! How is it that water is a liquid? As a chemist, I can explain that it's all down to 'hydrogen bonding' pulling the molecules of water to associate closely together, thus forming a liquid at normal temperatures. Is this a coincidence?

Another amazing feature of water is seen in its solid form—ice.

It is a matter of scientific fact that, as liquids are cooled, they become more dense (meaning that, for a given mass of the liquid, it takes up less space as it cools, because the molecules move more slowly and so huddle more closely together).

Liquids are at their densest just before they freeze—but NOT water! We find that water becomes more and more dense as it cools as far as 4 degrees centigrade; however, as it cools further, it becomes less dense. So water is at its densest at 4 degrees.

Now, if this were not the case, we would not be here. The rain would not be falling, the waves would not be pounding, and the river would not be flowing. If water were like all other liquids, ice would not float and, as a consequence, rivers, lakes, ponds and seas would freeze from the bottom upwards; once frozen, it is unlikely they would ever thaw—life in the waters would be impossible and intelligent life on earth would not happen. However, ice floats! Beneath the ice, the fish and other sea life can happily continue. The densest water sinks to the bottom of the seas and so the oceans never completely freeze! Is this a coincidence?

THE MOON

Now, let's move up a little and consider the moon, our only major satellite. It is about 16% of the earth's mass, orbiting our planet once a month at a distance of about 240,000 miles. So, what's special about the moon? We are familiar with the effect the moon has on the oceans and seas; its gravitational pull on the surface of the earth moves the waters and causes the tides we experience twice each day. The moon is also helpful in providing a measure of reflected sunlight on the earth during the night—it has also perhaps been useful for thousands of years in inspiring many romantic evenings! These are all interesting, but not necessary to our existence—

but if the moon were not where it is, we would not be here to observe it, for it is performing one vital function.

The earth is a spinning globe orbiting the sun in partnership with its smaller satellite. As the earth spins on its axis, it is tilted at an angle of 23 degrees. Because of this, at one part of our circuit around the sun, the northern hemisphere is tilted towards the sun, giving rise to our summer; at the opposite end of our circuit, the northern hemisphere is tilted away from the sun, creating our winter—and in between, we have spring and autumn. (The opposite, of course, is the case for the southern hemisphere.)

The seasons are of great use in nature, providing the necessary cycles for plant and crop growth. If the earth were not at 23 degrees but were instead vertical, the equatorial regions would be hot barren deserts and the northern and southern regions uninhabitably cold.

But here is the vital role of the moon! Without its pull on the earth, our planet's rotation on its axis would become unstable—we would 'wobble', rather like a child's spinning top as it slows down—and intelligent life would be impossible as vast tidal waves spilt continually over the land mass.

As things are, at 240,000 miles and 16% of the mass of the earth, it is 'just right' to keep us stable. Is this a coincidence?

THE SUN

Let's move up a little further and consider the sun, a massive thermonuclear fusion reactor converting hydrogen atoms into helium atoms by forcing them together at twenty million degrees centigrade. This reaction releases massive amounts of energy which pour out from its surface in the form of light and heat. The surface of the sun is somewhat cooler than the centre at only 6,000 degrees. As the blast of heat moves through space, its energy spreads and cools, until at ninety-three million miles further on, it reaches the earth and warms our planet to an average of fifteen degrees—just perfect for water-based life. Is this a coincidence?

Another feature of the sun is that it emits huge amounts of very harmful radiation (for example, gamma rays). These are lethal. Any organism exposed to such radiation will not survive for very long—in fact, under such conditions, life as we know it could never even begin! While we are grateful for the light and heat which are necessary for life, we do not want the gamma rays as they would kill us. Well, here is another amazing fact: the ozone layer in our upper atmosphere allows the heat and light through, but filters out the gamma rays—how about that?

JUPITER

Moving further up and out—we are so thankful for Jupiter. But for Jupiter, we would not be here. The solar system's fifth planet lies beyond the asteroid belt some 480 million miles from the sun and is considerably more massive than the earth—in fact you could fit over 1,000 planets the size of earth inside Jupiter. Now it is Jupiter's mass that is so vital to life on earth.

As well as the eight planets in our solar system, there are hundreds of thousands of smaller 'rocks' orbiting the sun, including asteroids, comets and meteors. While the orbits of the planets are regular and known, the orbits of many of these other bodies are not so, and, from time to time, will be on collision orbits with each other and with the planets themselves. It would only take a moderately sized space rock (a mile or so in diameter) to collide with our planet to bring an end to human existence.

What is it that keeps us relatively safe from this? Jupiter! Jupiter is so massive, its effect is to attract such rocks (which might otherwise hit the earth) to itself. In a way we could call Jupiter the 'goalkeeper' of the solar system. In July of 1994, we were able to observe Jupiter in action as a comet named Shoemaker-Levy slammed into the giant planet.

Who would have thought that such a distant planet could be of such a help to us here on earth?

Well, there are just a few 'coincidences' without which we would not be here. So, what do they tell us? Are they just cosmic flukes?

There is a scientific principle known as the 'anthropic principle' and, put simply, it states that, although the universe appears to have been finely tuned and designed for us, we only observe these things because the coincidences happen. If they hadn't happened, we would not be here; but, because they did (fantastic as they may seem), we are here! In the end it simply is coincidence. For those wishing to delve further into this theory, the Wikipedia web site has a very helpful summary.[2]

There is, however, an alternative. In much the same way that God sets the universe as a banner to shout out his existence to us, he also ordered the circumstances we are discovering to make that banner even clearer.

In much the same way that God sets the universe as a banner to shout out his existence to us, he also ordered the circumstances we are discovering to make that banner even clearer.

The Apostle Paul, while preaching in a city that had no knowledge of the true God, uses the argument of circumstances as a pointer to God. He tells the crowds:

> We are bringing you the good news, telling you to turn from these worthless things [idol worship] to the living God, who made heaven and earth and sea and everything in them. In the past, he let all nations go their own way. Yet he has not left himself without testimony: He has shown kindness by giving you rain from heaven and crops in their seasons; he provided you with plenty

of food and fills your hearts with joy.[3]

Paul's argument here is interesting: creation—that is, the universe—tells us that God is great, powerful and eternal; but the circumstances he has set in place tell us that he is kind, and he cares for us! This 'pointer' takes us a stage further: God is not only awesome and transcendent, he is close at hand and he cares for us.

1   *A Brief History* of Time, p125
2   www.en.wikipedia.org/wiki/anthropic_principle
3   Acts 14:15–17

Coincidence

Craving

Wherever you travel throughout the world, you will find a 'sense of God' in the heart of humankind. Every nation has its concept of, and ideas about, God or gods. This has always been the case throughout history; human beings are worshipping beings.

The three great monotheistic religions of the world, Judaism, Christianity and Islam, all trace their roots back to early Middle Eastern civilization. No matter where you look at the history of the nations, every culture, every tribe, has its concept of the divine.

Even today, whenever contact is made with a hitherto-unknown tribe, whether in the Amazon or in parts of Africa, the people there are found already to have fully-formed ideas of a great Creator whom they seek to worship and serve.

Although those views of the divine are very diverse—pantheists would say god is everything, Hindus would say there are many gods, Christians, Jews and Muslims say there is but one God (although they differ as to his character)—still we cannot escape the glaring fact that human beings are worshipping beings.

ATHEIST WISHES FOR GOD

The famous atheistic philosopher, Jean-Paul Sartre, wrote, 'That God does not exist, I cannot deny ...' So far, so good. This is classical atheism in typical form (and note Sartre's honesty in not saying 'There is *probably* no God ...'!).

However, he continues, 'That my very being cries out for God, I cannot forget!'[1]

How very interesting, how very honest—a famous philosopher declaring his atheism, yet not ashamed to admit his craving for the God he denies.

Blaise Pascal, the French mathematician and philosopher, put the matter very wonderfully when he said: 'There is a God-shaped vacuum in the heart of every man which cannot be filled by any created thing, but only by God the creator …'[2]

How do we account for this universal 'sense of God'?

Of all the animal life on planet earth, it is humankind alone that stops and ponders the divine. It is humankind alone that seeks out and strives to find God. It is humankind alone that seeks to please and to serve God. People pray, build great structures costing vast sums of money and costing (certainly in times past) many lives, search sacred scriptures and writings—they debate, they probe, they think … All this is unique to humans. I know of no piggy prayer meetings, no wildebeest worship meetings, no bovine Bible study groups!

> **Of all the animal life on planet earth, it is humankind alone that stops and ponders the divine.**

My dog, Jess, very rarely thinks above or beyond the

timing of her next meal. If I chat with her about the universe and the latest scientific theories in cosmology, she wags her tale. Of course, I cannot prove it, but I doubt very much she has any concern about her soul or her eternal wellbeing when she meets her maker—these things are human things, and the question is … why?

A BIT ABOUT DAWKINS

Atheistic philosophers have several theories which are variations on the same theme. Dawkins has an excellent chapter in his book *The God Delusion* where he seriously and honestly attempts to deal with this matter from a Darwinian perspective.[3] Read the chapter for yourself by all means, but here is a hopefully honest summary—his view is pretty contorted, but where the existence of God is ruled out as a nonstarter, then some other possibility must be found!

Dawkins's view is that belief in God may be likened to the action of moths flying into a lighted candle; a sort of 'unfortunate by product' of something which has great use to the moth. Moths will use the moon as a guidance system at night and often fly towards it to get their bearings—mistaking a lighted candle for the moon is a somewhat unfortunate by product of this helpful navigation aid. From this example, the following is argued: the children of early man would survive better if they believed 'without question' the things their elders told them, passing on the accumulated experience for survival from previous generations. This is very obviously helpful when it comes to instructions such as 'Don't eat that, it is poisonous' or 'Don't go near that animal, it will bite you'— following such instructions will aid a child's survival, while the type of child who does not follow his elders' instructions would tend to 'die out'. Thus, it is argued, Darwinianism selects out for survival those offspring who believe implicitly the things their parents tell them.

An unfortunate by-product of this, however, is that children also came to believe those things which were not helpful—including 'religious ideas'. But how did such 'religious ideas' arise in the first place? Well, it is argued, they came from an innate need to explain things and answer the question, 'Where has it come from?' Hence, early people made up these religious stories and passed them on to their gullible children.

Another intriguing proposal in Dawkins' chapter is that belief in God is a kind of 'misfiring' of certain 'data-processing' areas of the brain. Here, examples given for such misfiring include falling in love! Dawkins alludes to anthropologist Helen Fisher as expressing romantic love being 'insane', while he himself asks, '… isn't the total exclusiveness we expect of spousal love positively weird?' However, its usefulness is seen in securing strong family units.

Putting these two theories together, Dawkins states, 'The equivalent of the moth's light compass reaction is the apparent irrational but useful habit of falling in love with one, and only one, member of the opposite sex. The misfiring by-product—equivalent to flying into the candle flame—is falling in love with Yahweh (or the Virgin Mary, or with a wafer, or with Allah).'

Well, I hope I have been accurate in conveying the essence of Dawkins' chapter, but doesn't it strike you as being a little bit desperate? Even Dawkins himself states, '... the useful gullibility of the child mind is only an example of the kind (his emphasis) of thing that might be the analogue of moths navigating by the moon or the stars.'[4]

Again, the well-known phrase, 'There are none so blind as those who will not see' comes readily to mind! The obvious is dismissed in favour of the obscure, all for the sake of a prejudiced mantra, 'There probably is no God!'

Is not the obvious reason for this universal God-consciousness simply this, that he really is there, and this craving is yet another powerful pointer to that fact?

The obvious is dismissed in favour of the obscure, all for the sake of a prejudiced mantra, 'There probably is no God!'

THE WONDER OF BEING HUMAN

The Bible points out very clearly that God made humans as the pinnacle of all his created works. Vast as the universe undoubtedly is, and search as you might, you will search in vain to find anything in all creation to surpass humankind. It is people alone who have been made 'in the image of God'. Since God has no physical form, it is clear that this image is spiritual, and so it is the souls of human beings. With our bodies we share much in common with the animal world— hunger, thirst, growth, procreation—but it is with our souls that we share much with the divine; we are creative, communicative, we plan, ponder and consider. These are part of the image of God in the human soul, which find only pale shadows in the animal kingdom.

Consider the creative capabilities of humans. What wonders we can design and build; what works of art we can create! This is the creative image of God. I am not a great drawer, but I can draw a passing likeness to our dog, Jess— but in ten years with us in our home, she has never drawn a picture of me, and she has never drawn a picture of any member of the family!

Animals may be said to have design capabilities—look at the nest a bird builds or the hive a bee produces—but the fact is, they are always the same; no bird branches out and builds a three-bedroomed nest with lounge, kitchen and utility room! It's always the same design.

Consider our communicative skills—language is an astonishing feature and mirrors the communicative image of God. Granted, animals can give mating and warning calls—

but these are an infinity away from what we are doing right now. I wrote my thoughts down and you are now reading them!

God is a God who plans, and that stamp is on us too. We plan our lives, our work, our leisure and pleasure. My dog plans nothing.

But the supreme consequence of the image of God in the human soul is this—we crave our Maker! God made us for many things, but supremely he made us to know him—and nothing in all creation truly satisfies apart from him. God, and God alone, can FILL the vacuum—it is a God-shaped vacuum.

Solomon wrote in the Bible: 'He [God] has also set eternity in the hearts of men.'[5]

Jesus Christ said: 'Now this is eternal life [real life]: that they may know you, the only true God …'[6]

Augustine, the great church leader of the fourth century, wrote: 'You have made us for yourself, and our hearts are restless until they rest in you.'[7]

This God-craving, far from being some sort of by-product or psychological defect, is yet another powerful pointer to the reality of the Divine Being!

Well, if there is a God, and he made us in his image and

made us to know him—why don't we know him? We begin to answer this question in our next chapter.

1 www.brainyquote.com/quotes/authors/j/jeanpaul_sarte_3.html
2 www.brainyquote.com/quotes/authore/b/blaise_pascal_6.html
3 *The God Delusion*, pp163-207
4 *The God Delusion*, p177
5 Ecclesiastes 3:11
6 John 17:3
7 *Confessions*; Augustine; Book 1, p1

Craving

Conscience

There is a lovely story concerning the great nineteenth-century Baptist preacher, Charles Spurgeon. Entering the church office for his usual Monday morning meeting with the church deacons, he found the men smoking their pipes. Shaking his generous frame and addressing the assembled group, he said, 'Gentlemen, have you no conscience about smoking your pipes this early in the morning?'

'Oh, sorry Mr Spugeon,' replied the chairman of the deacons, as each man sheepishly put out his pipe.

Spurgeon is then reputed to have sat at the head of the table. Taking out his own pipe he filled it with tobacco, lit it and drew heavily on it.

While all the deacons looked perplexed, the brave chairman addressed the preacher: 'But Mr Spurgeon ... I thought you said we were not to smoke?'

Drawing again on his pipe, Spurgeon gave a smile, leaned forward and said, 'I did not say you were not to smoke; I merely asked if you had a conscience about it—I have not, therefore I shall smoke.'

Whether or not the story is true, it is one we can relate to!

We have this thing in us called 'the conscience'. It seems to be a set of internal traffic lights operating to guide us through the actions taken day by day:

Green—Go ahead, no problem here.

Red—STOP, reverse out, don't say it, do it, think it! Amber—Now, not too sure here; proceed with caution and be ready to stop!

The conscience is a really useful function of the mind. It is wise not to go against it. Jiminy Cricket's advice to Pinocchio was: 'Always let your conscience be your guide.'

The question is, where did this come from? What evolutionary advantage does the conscience possibly give if it is a matter of 'survival of the fittest'? Surely the ultimate survivors would be those who were hard-hearted, with little conscience, looking after number one!

But we find today everybody has a conscience. Granted, it seems to operate at different levels in different people—or even at different levels in the same person at different times—but we cannot escape the conscience and its often powerful effect on our lives.

We cannot escape the conscience and its often powerful effect on our lives.

There are remarkable stories of criminals turning themselves in at police stations, confessing crimes which nobody had a clue they had committed—and why? They could no longer live with their consciences, raging and accusing!

As a practical joke in the nineteenth century, Sir Arthur Conan Doyle sent telegrams to twelve of London's leading socialites of the day; the telegram simply said 'Flee, all is revealed!' Conan Doyle had nothing on them—it was a practical joke—but, consciences suddenly ablaze, seven of those men left the country!

The conscience is useful, but not always reliable; with some it can be too sensitive, holding them back from doing harmless or legitimate things.

MALFUNCTION

With others, years and years of abuse have seared the conscience and virtually shut it down to such an extent that individuals can carry out terrible atrocities, wrecking many lives, including their own. Our prisons hold many such men and women. I remember visiting the youth wing of a prison and talking with a group of about twelve young offenders about the conscience—how we all have one, what its uses are and what its source is—when one young man interrupted me, saying: 'I don't have a conscience.'

His cold stare and hard expression were shocking. Here was a young man who had made every effort to shut down this wonderful mechanism—for him, the traffic light was almost always on green. I don't know where he is today—but with a hardened conscience he will bring pain to others and, ultimately, to himself.

There is the story of the airliner flying over the Andes Mountains in the dark of night; the ground proximity alarm calls out a warning: 'Pull up! Pull up! Pull up!' The pilot and co-pilot are heard to check their instruments and can find no reason for the warning. Moments later the same siren voice blasts out: 'Pull up! Pull up! Pull up!' Again, checks are carried out and no problem is found. Once more, the siren is heard: this time only one, 'Pull up …!' as the pilot turns off the siren with the words, 'Aw shut up, gringo!'

Moments later the airliner slams into the mountainside—and all on board are killed.

It is dangerous thing to override the conscience.

But let me ask again: where did it come from? This mechanism seems to be unique to humankind—an internal reference to right and wrong.

When Mr Fox raids the chicken run and eats Chicken Licken, he is doing what foxes do—he does not skulk home to Mrs Fox, wailing with conscience-stricken grief, 'Oh, what have I done?' No, he has no conscience about the havoc he caused in the chicken run and, furthermore, he will do it again given the chance.

Let me come back to our dog, Jess, mentioned in an earlier chapter. She can do things she knows she shouldn't do—maybe she ate the Sunday joint left on the kitchen table. When I come in I know she has done something wrong! She cannot hide it; head down, she makes no eye contact …

This is not a conscience operating, but a fear of

consequences—she knows there is trouble ahead for her! If Jess knew she would never be found out, she would repeat the same actions time after time. Left entirely to themselves, our pets would revert fully back to type and begin to operate like every other wild animal.

WHERE DID IT COME FROM?

So, we have this conscience—an internal reference to right and wrong that curbs many of our actions; where has it come from? It seems there are three options:

Firstly, the conscience has evolved.

The suggestion is that there is some evolutionary advantage gained from early people having a conscience. However, it is difficult to imagine, in the savage reality of 'survival of the fittest', what possible advantage a conscience might have brought. Surely it is the hard, callous, early man who triumphs over the softer-hearted rival? There are books which propound this theory, but I can see no merit in it. Again, Dawkins makes a valid attempt in his book[1], but only manages to tackle the issue of morality—whereas conscience does so much more than that.

Secondly, it is a matter of environment and human conditioning.

A child brought up in soft, caring surroundings will, generally speaking, have a tender conscience and care for others as he or she has been cared for. Conversely, the child raised in harsh, adverse or cruel circumstances becomes a hard, harsh child with little care or feelings for others.

> **While it is certainly true that a young conscience can be shaped by environment, it does not answer the question as to where it came from.**

While it is certainly true that a young conscience can be shaped by environment, it does not answer the question as to where it came from. Neither does it account for the fact that children raised in harsh environments can have very tender consciences while those raised in caring surroundings can be very hard—environment has an influence, but it is not the source!

The third option is the logical one—it is yet another 'powerful pointer' to the existence of God.

Again, to refer to the atheist, Sartre: "The existentialist thinks it very distressing that God does not exist, because all possibility of finding values in a heaven of ideas disappears along with him; there can no longer be any ultimate good ..."[2]

Yet our consciences tell us that there is indeed 'ultimate good', pointing to the ultimate being—God!

Creation tells us God is there; all-powerful and eternal.

Circumstances reveal God is not only there, but he cares for us.

Craving tells us we were made to know God and that only he will truly satisfy us.

Conscience tells us two things—it tells us something about God, and something about ourselves:

Firstly, it tells us something about God. He is the ultimate 'right'. Again, this is part of the image of God unique to human beings. We have an innate sense of right and wrong, of justice and fair play, because God our creator put that stamp within us—it is a reflection of his rightness, justice and equity. God is the ultimate right, and he has written a sense of that on our souls: The Apostle Paul takes up this point in writing to the church at Rome, '… they show that the requirements of the law [of God] are written on their hearts, their consciences [my emphasis] also bearing witness, and their thoughts now accusing, now even defending them.'[3]

Here, the conscience either defends or accuses in accordance with the law of God written on our hearts!

But secondly, it is clear also from this statement by Paul that we learn from our consciences much about ourselves—we are far from what God would have us be. We are not 'right'; we are often wrong and for this our conscience condemns us and puts us to shame.

This now gives an answer to the question with which we ended the last chapter: 'If there is a God, and he made us to know him—why don't we know him?'

And the answer from our conscience is clear: we are not good enough! He is perfect and we are not, and so there is a moral rift between us and our maker.

Isaiah, the Old Testament prophet, put it this way: 'Your iniquities [moral failures] have separated you from your God.'[4]

Our consciences, then, are yet another powerful pointer to the existence of this awesome Being—God!

All these pointers are really beginning to stack up and have almost become that 'sign in the sky' that many say they need—well here it is! (Again, there are none as blind as those who will not see!)

But, if this all-powerful God, who cares for me and made me to know him, can't be known because he is pure and I am not—what's the answer? Can anything be done?

Thankfully, yes—and it begins to unfold in our next powerful pointer.

1   *The God Delusion*; p211
2   *Existentialism and Humanism*; Jean-Paul Sartre; Methuen Young Books; 1948
3   Romans 2:15
4   Isaiah 59:2

Conscience

Canon—the Bible

OK, so you are still awake! We have arrived at our fifth powerful pointer to the existence of God, each beginning with the letter 'C'—and you've spotted that Bible starts with a 'B'!

Another name for the Bible is 'the Canon of Scripture', so let's use that word 'Canon' and we are still in with the flow! (Canon refers, in this instance, to a collection of writings.)

There are so many fantastic books in the world telling many wonderful stories; high on that list would be JRR Tolkien's *The Lord of the Rings*. What an amazing world he creates, what strong characters, what a story—but it is just that—a story—originating in the mind of Tolkien.

Then there's the Narnia series—the world through the wardrobe; *Star Wars*, the story of a galaxy 'far, far away'— again, great stories; but fictitious, made up.

But what of the Bible? Often described as 'The greatest story ever told', what a story it is! Have you read it?

IN A NUTSHELL

The outline is stunningly simple: God creates a universe—but the central focus is a tiny planet called 'earth'; there he sets the pinnacle of his created order, 'humankind'—he makes humans with the capacity to know and enjoy fellowship with him—but the first man exercises his 'freedom of choice' and rebels against his maker. The result is that he is cut off from God's immediate presence and condemned to be for ever away from him—the man and his descendants are now 'dead' to God, aimless in their lives, destined to die physically, and fearful of a judgement to come!

But God will not be thwarted in his purpose and he reveals his eternal plan to rescue his fallen image-bearers—he will send a Saviour! Throughout what is known as the Old Testament, more and more details are given of this Saviour—and eventually, when he arrives—incredibly, he is God himself who becomes a man (ah, God the Son, that is—not the Father, not the Spirit … but that's another story!). Jesus Christ, this God-man, lives a perfect life and then dies as if he had not lived a perfect life. We are told he lived that life as our representative—then he died as our representative; taking the judgement we deserve.

> **God will not be thwarted in his purpose and he reveals his eternal plan to rescue his fallen image-bearers—he will send a Saviour!**

Death had a problem. It could not keep Jesus because his record was clear—morally perfect, perfectly 'right'—so death released him.

The Bible tells us that God can forgive us and we can be restored to him if we trust the Saviour.

That is the story—the greatest story ever told!

Is it true?

To help, let's examine two objective pieces of evidence that will point to God being the author of the Bible—and if that is shown to be the case, we do two things; we have another powerful pointer that God exists and we show that its message is true!

UNITY

The first piece of evidence is the unity of the book.

It is a fact that the Bible was written over a period of some 2,000 years, using forty different human authors. The great majority of these authors never met one another and were from vastly differing backgrounds—each wrote a piece of what we now call the Bible, sixty-six different books; thirty-nine before Jesus, twenty-seven during and after.

The amazing thing is this, when these sixty-six books are brought together, we find ONE unfolding story (which was so very briefly outlined above). The pieces fit! There was no collusion—indeed, there could have been none! It is not as if these authors got together and, over a period of five or ten years, conferred and produced the Bible—they never met; death itself separated them!

Contrary to the often-touted line 'The Bible is full of

contradictions and errors', it is not—none that stands up to close scrutiny, anyway.

So, how do we account for this: the period of two thousand years, forty authors, one unfolding seamless story? There is only one logical conclusion; one supreme author who oversaw all those human authors—and that supreme author must have been alive throughout the two thousand years.

The Bible's direct claim is that its ultimate author is God himself: 'All Scripture is God-breathed ...'[1]

The Bible claims that God oversaw the writings of each human author: 'Above all, you must understand that no prophecy of Scripture came about by the prophet's own interpretation. For prophecy never had its origin in the will of man, but men spoke from God as they were carried along by the Holy Spirit.'[2]

FULFILLED PROPHECY

The second piece of evidence is Bible prophecy.

Interspersed throughout the Bible's storyline are hundreds of prophecies—predictions of future events. These prophecies are not at all vague, but are detailed predictions of specific events, quite unlike anything else that could be encountered. There are so-called prophecies by men such as Nostradamus, which claim to be specific and detailed, but then clearly fail in their fulfilment. Some equate Nostradamus' prediction of someone called 'Hister' with Hitler.[3] But that is just not good enough! Hister is NOT Hitler—the names are quite different!

Bible prophecy is specific, detailed and verifiable.

For example, in the details of the coming Saviour foretold throughout the Old Testament, there are hundreds of very specific prophecies, all verifiably fulfilled in the person of Jesus Christ. For a detailed analysis of these, the reader is directed to Josh McDowell's excellent book *Evidence that Demands a Verdict*.[4]

However, in this brief section, we focus on a particularly striking prophecy concerning the secular history of the world.

The prophet Daniel was among the Jewish exiles taken captive by Nebuchadnezzar in approximately 600 BC. Daniel rose to become a high ranking official in the Babylonian empire, but he stayed loyal to the Lord his God. God gave to Daniel many dreams and visions in which he was shown the future course of world history. In particular, in chapter 2, while Daniel was still a young man (around 575 BC), God showed him that following the end of the Babylonian empire there would be three more major empires. Daniel was also given details as to the character of these empires. At the fall of the fourth empire, Daniel was shown there would be a fragmentation of that empire into a multiplicity of kingdoms.

History shows the clear fulfilment of that prophecy, and with astonishing accuracy. Following the Babylonian empire, there came the Medo-Persian Empire; this was followed by the Greek empire, which, in turn, was followed by the Roman Empire. The fall of the Roman Empire brought about a multiplicity of kingdoms which, in turn, explains the nations of Europe today!

Now, sceptics confronted with such stunning prophecy draw the following conclusion: Daniel must have been written after the events that he supposedly predicted! But, the latest possible date that even a sceptic can assign to Daniel is the second century BC, simply because there are scrolls of Daniel in existence which can be dated from that time. So, even for the sceptic, the rise and fall of Rome and its fragmentation into many kingdoms still has to be explained!

The stronger evidence, however, is that Daniel was written by Daniel in the sixth century BC.[5]

Who, but God, can know the future with such unerring precision?

The Bible states that God is eternal and that he inhabits eternity; he is 'yesterday and today and for ever',[6] he is all dates and not confined by time or space. He knows the future because he is there already—but, more than that, he knows the future because he has planned the future and is working out his purposes.

Secular history only has real relevance as it relates to God and his purposes; so, to return to Daniel, God told Daniel that, during that final empire, he would set up his kingdom that would endure for ever. It was, of course, during the days of the Roman Empire that Jesus was born in Bethlehem of Judea!

Bible prophecy is a powerful pointer that the Bible is God's book and that God exists!

In the next chapter we will take a closer look at the Bible's central character.

1   2 Timothy 3:16
2   2 Peter 1:20–21
3   Nostradamus; Century 2; Quatrain 24
4   Josh McDowell; *Evidence that Demands a Verdict*; Campus Crusade for Christ
5   See *Daniel*; EJ Young; Banner of Truth, Edinburgh (ISBN 0-85151-154-6)
6   Psalm 90:2; Hebrews 13:8

Christ

Christ is a title, the Greek equivalent of the Hebrew 'Messiah', and means 'anointed one' or 'promised one'. Through the thirty-nine books of the Old Testament, more and more information was given about the Christ who was to be sent into the world—all these promises (and there were hundreds of them) are fulfilled in the person of Jesus of Nazareth, born in Bethlehem of Judea in around 4 BC.

Not many would seriously dispute that a person known as Jesus the Christ lived on this planet some 2,000 years ago. In writing one of the biographies of his life, Luke is very careful to set down verifiable historical details. In the introduction to his account Luke tells us:

> Many have undertaken to draw up an account of the things that have been fulfilled amongst us, just as they were handed down to us by those who from the first were eye-witnesses and servants of the word. Therefore, since I myself have carefully investigated everything from the beginning, it seemed good also to me to write an orderly account for you, most excellent Theophilus, so that you may know the certainty of the things you have been taught.[1]

The account Luke wrote to Theophilus we have in the Bible as the third Gospel—the Gospel according to Luke.

Luke is clearly a careful historian. He tells us that at the birth of Jesus, Augustus was the Caesar, that Quirinius was governor of Syria, and that a census was being taken of the Roman world. As Jesus starts his public ministry thirty years later, Luke informs us that Tiberius was in his fifteenth year, that Pilate was governor of Judea, and that Herod, Philip and Lysanias were Tetrarchs of Galilee, Iturea and Abilene respectively.

UNAMBIGUOUS

Apart from the Bible, several secular historians of the time write about Jesus the Christ, none of whom were sympathetic to Christianity. Here are excerpts from two of them; first of all, the Roman historian Tacitus, writing about the burning of Rome in Nero's time:

> To suppress this rumour, Nero fabricated scapegoats—and punished with every refinement the notoriously depraved Christians (as they were popularly called). Their originator, Christ, had been executed in Tiberius' reign by the governor of Judea, Pontius Pilatus.[2]

The Jewish historian, Josephus, also referred to Jesus on several occasions. Here is one:

> At this time there was a wise man called Jesus, and his conduct was good, and he was known to be virtuous. Many people among the Jews and the other nations became his disciples. Pilate condemned him to be crucified and to die. But those who had become

his disciples did not abandon his discipleship. They reported that he had appeared to them three days after his crucifixion and that he was alive.[3]

There is little doubt that Jesus existed. The question for debate is 'Who was he?'

This is not only a modern debate, but one that raged at the time of his public ministry also; for example, Mark tells us, 'Jesus and his disciples went on to the villages around Caesarea Philippi. On the way he asked them, "Who do people say I am?"

'They replied, "Some say John the Baptist; others say Elijah; and still others, one of the prophets."

'"But what about you?" he asked. "Who do you say that I am?" Peter answered, "You are the Christ."'[4]

There are many other examples in the Gospels describing people's divided opinions as to who Jesus was—but there are no doubts with respect to his claims!

For example, at the very climax of the gospel story when Jesus was on trial for his very life before the assembled Jewish high court—the question was put directly and unambiguously to him by the High Priest: 'Are you the Christ, the Son of the Blessed One?'

The reply Jesus gave sealed his death sentence that night: 'I am,' said Jesus. 'And you will see the Son of Man sitting at the right hand of the Mighty One and coming on the clouds of heaven.'[5]

There is nothing ambiguous here! Even the title he often took for himself, 'the Son of Man', had powerfully divine implications rooted in Daniel's seventh chapter.

Going back from the incident with the High Priest by a few hours, we find Jesus with his disciples; and after three years, some of them are clearly still confused as to exactly who he is. Consider the words of Philip, who asked, 'Lord, show us the Father and that will be enough for us.'

Jesus answered, 'Don't you know me, Philip, even after I have been among you such a long time? Anyone who has seen me has seen the Father.'[6]

That is a truly outrageous statement! In effect, Jesus was saying, 'If you have seen me, you have seen God!' Can you imagine anyone ever making such a claim? Jesus made it.

There is no doubt that his enemies understood his claims, but they rejected them vigorously and treated his statements as blasphemy. For example, in debating with a group of hostile Jews Jesus tells them, 'Your father Abraham rejoiced at the thought of seeing my day; he saw it and was glad.'

"You are not yet fifty years old," the Jews said to him, "and you have seen Abraham!"

"I tell you the truth," Jesus answered, "before Abraham was born, I am!"

At this they picked up stones to stone him ...[7]

Those Jews understood exactly what Jesus was saying. Although Abraham had died 2,000 years earlier, he had seen Jesus and Jesus had seen him!

On another occasion, also speaking to a crowd of religious Jews, Jesus says, "I and the Father are one." Again, the Jews picked up stones to stone him, but Jesus said to them, "I have shown you many great miracles from the Father. For which of these do you stone me?"

"We are not stoning you for any of these," replied the Jews, "but for blasphemy, because you, a mere man, claim to be God."[8]

So, Jesus existed; he claimed to be God and his enemies understood his claim; his own disciples (although somewhat slow on the uptake) came to believe it—but, is it true?

We can certainly say this, whoever he was, that no life has affected the course of human history more than this man's!

One writer very powerfully put it this way:

> Here is a man who was born in an obscure village, the child of a peasant woman. He grew up in another village. He worked in a carpenter shop until he was thirty, and then for three years was an itinerant

preacher. He never owned a home. He never wrote a book. He never held an office. He never had a family. He never went to college. He never put his foot inside a major city. He never travelled 200 miles from the place where he was born. He never did one of the things that usually accompany greatness. He had no credentials but himself ... While still a young man, the tide of popular opinion turned against him. His friends ran away, one of them denied him. He was turned over to his enemies. He went through the mockery of a trial. He was nailed to a cross between two thieves. While he was dying, his executioners gambled for the only piece of property he had on earth—his coat. When he was dead he was taken down and laid in a borrowed grave through the pity of a friend.

Nineteen centuries have come and gone, and today he is the centrepiece of the human race and the leader of the column of progress. I am far within the mark when I say that all the armies that ever marched, all the navies that ever sailed, all the parliaments that ever sat and all the kings who ever reigned, put together, have not affected the life of man upon this planet as powerfully as has that one solitary life.[9]

Jesus Christ has split time in two; we write the date each day with reference to his life!

But, if it is true, what was the point? Why would God become a man and come to this planet?

He claimed not only to be God, but also the way to God:

'I am the way, and the truth and the life. No one comes to the Father except through me.'[10]

He claims to be the giver of eternal life!

'My sheep listen to my voice; I know them, and they follow me. I give them eternal life, and they shall never perish ...'[11]

He claimed that his death, which was no accident or shock to him, would be as a payment for humankind's sinful rebellion—he was going to die in our place.

He claimed that his death, which was no accident or shock to him, would be as a payment for humankind's sinful rebellion—he was going to die in our place; paying our debt to a perfect, holy God of justice: 'For even the Son of Man did not come to be served, but to serve, and to give his life as a ransom for many.'[12]

DRAWING IT ALL TOGETHER

By way of summary, let's put it all briefly together:

Who is Jesus?

He is God the Son. There is one God but three persons revealed—the Father, the Son, and the Holy Spirit.

Two thousand years ago, it is the Son who left heaven and became a man, while remaining fully God. He came as one person with two natures, being fully human yet also fully divine.

His purpose was clear. It was to take away our biggest problem—our moral failure and rebellion (what the Bible calls 'sin')—from before a holy God. If not properly dealt with, this sin would sink us under eternal judgement.

To accomplish this, Jesus did two things: he lived a perfect life for us, and he died a perfect death for us.

Firstly, to know God and in order for me to get to heaven, I need a clean or 'right' life, and I don't have one. Moreover, by my own efforts, I never will have one—but Jesus lived that life for me!

Secondly, my failure deserves an eternal punishment from God, which the Bible calls hell. Whatever hell is, it is a place to avoid. Jesus spoke more of hell than he ever spoke of heaven and he did this to warn us. Remarkably, to save us from this place, Jesus went there himself—for Calvary, the place where Jesus died on a Roman cross, was the equivalent of hell. It was there that God the Father poured out on his own Son the punishment that we, as sinners, deserve!

Ponder this: God, the great and righteous judge, rightly

condemns us to hell—we are the rebels; then goes there himself in the person of Jesus and pays our debt.

As Jesus dies on the cross, he declares, 'It is finished!' The expression recorded in the Greek language is a very rich one and means 'finished' in the sense of 'completely accomplished'!

The Welsh poet, Islwyn wrote:

> It is finished Jesus said,
> as he bowed his sacred head
> All that God did ever plan,
> was accomplished for man.

As we noted previously, death hangs on to sinners—but it could not hang on to Jesus. He had no sin. As he said he would, on the third day he rose from the grave.

Task completed. Job done!

OK, but two thousand years later, how do we benefit from this?

The words of Jesus Christ are very clear and unambiguous; if we turn to him in faith, we can be restored to God, we can know eternal life, and we are guaranteed a place in heaven.

Then Jesus declared, 'I am the bread of life. He who comes to me will never go hungry, and he who believes in me will never be thirsty … All that the Father gives me will come to me, and whoever comes to me I will never drive away. For I have come down from heaven not to do my will but to do the will of him who sent me. And this is the will of him who sent me, that I shall lose none of all that he has given me, but raise them up at the last day. For my Father's will is that everyone who looks to the Son and believes in him shall have eternal life, and I will raise him up at the last day.'[13]

But, how does this happen?!

Perhaps our last chapter will be of help!

1   Luke 1:1–4
2   *Annals of Imperial Rome*; Tacitus; Penguin Books; p365
3   Josephus, *Jewish Antiquities*, A18
4   Mark 8:27–29
5   Mark 14:61–62
6   John 14:8–9
7   John 8:56–59
8   John 10:30–33
9   Anonymous but famous quote
10 John 14:6
11 John 10:27–28
12 Mark 10:45
13 John 6:35, 37–40

Christian experience

The first five chapters have examined a series of 'powerful pointers' towards the existence of God. These pointers are things we can see, touch, analyse and relate to—in that sense we may call them 'objective evidences'. With the careful examination of objective evidences, we can come to a deductive conclusion—this is good, scientific reasoning.

From such reasoning, the former atheist, Anthony Flew, changed his mind and has become a 'theist'—that is, he now believes there is indeed a God. Remember his words quoted in the introduction? 'In short, my discovery of the Divine has been a pilgrimage of reason and not of faith.'

With objective deduction, we can say, 'Seeing is believing.'

But, such deductive reasoning from objective facts has not, and indeed cannot by itself, bring us into a personal encounter with God. For that, we must enter the realm of the subjective—faith, feeling, and personal experience. In this realm it is not 'seeing is believing' but 'believing is seeing'!

OBJECTIVE AND SUBJECTIVE

The essential bridge between the objective and the subjective is the person of Jesus Christ. Here, with him, there is both objective reality (history, the Bible) and subjective experience. We meet the risen, living Christ who brings us to an encounter with God. Joseph Hart, a Christian leader and hymn writer of the eighteenth century, once said, 'True

> **'True religion is "more than notion"; something must be known and felt.'**

religion is "more than notion"; something must be known and felt.'[1]

And that is exactly it!

It is notion; objective facts, facts that may be investigated; but it is more than notion—with those objective facts comes that subjective experimental reality of meeting God himself!

So far, Anthony Flew has become a theist through objective observation and deduction, but he has not ruled out the possibility of the subjective; he says towards the end of his book:

> The discovery of phenomena like the laws of nature ... has led scientists, philosophers and others to accept the existence of an infinitely intelligent Mind. Some claim to have made contact with that Mind. I have not—yet. But who knows what could happen next? Someday I might hear a Voice that says, 'Can you hear me now?'[2]

That which Flew says has not yet happened to him has, in fact, happened to many and is our final and ultimately conclusive piece of evidence—Christian experience. It is faith, but not 'a leap in the dark', rather a faith based firmly on objective truths; the things we have been considering already in this book—creation, circumstances, craving, conscience, Canon and, supremely, Christ.

For the great majority who come to a personal, subjective encounter with God, it is built on these objective considerations. But, it must be said, this is not necessarily so; I know of individuals who had a subjective encounter with God who only afterwards were able to put in place the objective structure with which to understand their experience—God is God, and as such can operate in a person's life as he likes!

So, how does it happen? Let me give you my story.

MY STORY

At the age of nineteen, I was studying for my degree in Chemistry at Cardiff University. At that particular point, if pushed, I would have called myself an atheist—I felt all the answers I needed were in the realms of science; a big bang and evolution seemed entirely plausible explanations for our existence.

However, after my first year, I went on a long summer holiday to Australia; my grandparents lived on the Gold Coast and my aunt and two cousins lived nearby in Brisbane. On arriving, I discovered that my two cousins (both lads about my age) had recently been converted to Christianity—their lives had been totally changed—and instead of playing in secular rock bands and following the lifestyle of most teenagers in Brisbane, they now played in a Christian band and followed the lifestyle prescribed by Jesus in the Gospels.

In spending time with them, I was able to observe something I had not really encountered close up before—real Christianity, as opposed to 'Religion'. They read the Bible and believed it, they prayed and expected answers—and their lives were clean and wholesome. There was a joy, peace and contentment that was plain to see.

I went to a service at their church, and, to be honest found, it very off-putting. The worship was pretty wild and some bizarre things were happening—I was not impressed. But I was impressed with the people, especially my cousins.

I bought a Bible and began to read from Genesis, but I couldn't make much of it. As I spent more time with my cousins, they told me the amazing story of Jesus and how it was he who had changed their lives. This same Jesus, they assured me, could change mine too—could it be true?

I had so many questions! What about evolution? What about a big bang? What about evil and the bad things that happen in the world? If there is a God, why doesn't he stop these things? (Yes, we have all asked those questions!)

All these questions were genuine and seemed to be a real blockage to my making any progress, until a wise Christian said to me: 'You know, you need to start with Jesus, get him in place, and all your questions will fall into place too.' That did help.

Two weeks before I was due to return home, I found myself again going to church—as I was about to go in, I remember pausing at the door as the thought struck me: I was a scientist—scientists conduct experiments, look at the results and finally they draw conclusions. So, I conducted my experiment. I prayed, 'God, if you are there it is obviously very important that I know. I have been told amazing things and I need to know if they are real—please, if you are there, let me know.'

It was not the greatest prayer ever prayed, but it was sincere—I meant it. I'm not sure to this day what the minister preached on, but, in the service, I became powerfully aware of the Being of God—that Awesome Clean Being. I was aware of my sinfulness, my moral failure—and then the story of Jesus! It was like watching a jigsaw puzzle come together before my eyes! My soul embraced the reality I now found myself believing—and I was saved, right where I sat.

The service concluded with a strong appeal for people who wanted to receive Christ as their Saviour to come forward for prayer. As the choir sang 'Amazing Grace', at the last verse—to the astonishment of my cousins—I went forward. But it wasn't my action of going forward that saved me; it was Jesus, and he had done it right where I was sitting!

More than thirty years have gone by. I graduated in chemistry, followed it up with a PhD, worked as a chemist for five years, then, at the age of thirty, felt the call of Christ to full-time Christian ministry where I have been ever since.

That's my story. It's similar to so many others. What's your story?

If you are still not 'there', what next?

Read the Gospels, prayerfully asking God to help you.

Attend a church where the Bible is believed and preached.

And please feel free to email me! andychristofides@googlemail.com

1   *Gadsby's Hymnal*, No 237
2   *There is a God*, p158

ABOUT DAY ONE:

Day One's threefold commitment:

- To be faithful to the Bible, God's inerrant, infallible Word;
- To be relevant to our modern generation;
- To be excellent in our publication standards.

I continue to be thankful for the publications of Day One. They are biblical; they have sound theology; and they are relevant to the issues at hand. The material is condensed and manageable while, at the same time, being complete—a challenging balance to find. We are happy in our ministry to make use of these excellent publications.

JOHN MACARTHUR, PASTOR-TEACHER, GRACE COMMUNITY CHURCH, CALIFORNIA

It is a great encouragement to see Day One making such excellent progress. Their publications are always biblical, accessible and attractively produced, with no compromise on quality. Long may their progress continue and increase!

JOHN BLANCHARD, AUTHOR, EVANGELIST AND APOLOGIST

Visit our web site for more information and
to request a free catalogue of our books.
www.dayone.co.uk

U.S. web site:
www.dayonebookstore.com